Common Core Lessons & Activities:
Ancient Greece

By Carole Marsh

Published by Gallopade International, Inc.

Printed in the U.S.A. (Peachtree City, Georgia)

TABLE OF CONTENTS

G: Includes Graphic Organizer

GO: Graphic Organizer is also available 8½'
download at www.gallopade.com/clie
(numbers above correspond to the gr

I0895167

Pericles & Alexander

Read the two texts and complete the activities.

Pericles was one of the most important and influential Greek statesmen and generals of Athens. He ruled during Athens' Golden Age, when the city and culture was at its greatest. The period when he led Athens is known as the "Age of Pericles."

Pericles had a tremendous impact on Athenian society. He helped turn the Delian League, a group of city-states, into an Athenian empire. Pericles created projects to rebuild Athens after many Persian invasions. He also led his people during the first two years of the Peloponnesian War.

Pericles was known for promoting the arts and literature of Athens. Because of his efforts, Athens became known as the educational and cultural center of the ancient Greek world. Pericles launched a project to build most of the structures that survive today on the Acropolis, including the magnificent Parthenon. This project added to the beauty of the city and provided jobs for the people of Athens.

Pericles believed strongly in Athenian democracy. He has even been called a "populist," one who sides with the people against the rulers and upper class.

---

1. On a separate sheet of paper, create a Venn diagram to compare and contrast Pericles and Alexander the Great.

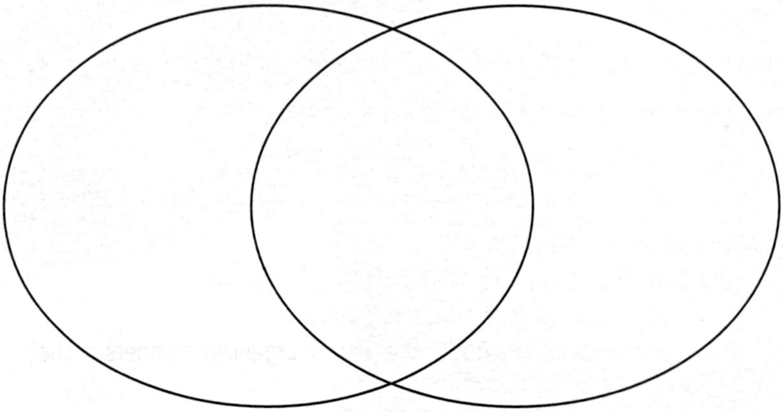

Alexander III was born in 356 B.C.E., over 100 years after Pericles. His father was King Phillip II of Macedon, a city-state in northern ancient Greece. The famous Greek philosopher Aristotle tutored Alexander until he was 16 years old.

Alexander became king of Macedon when his father died. He wanted to use his strong kingdom and experienced army to expand his kingdom into Asia. Alexander saw that the Persian Empire was growing weak. He used his superior army to free areas of Greek people ruled by the Persians. He then went on to conquer the entire Persian Empire without a single defeat in battle, earning the name "Alexander the Great."

He founded many cities that are named after him, including Alexandria in Egypt. By age 30, Alexander had created one of the largest empires of the ancient world. His empire stretched from the Ionian Sea just west of Greece to the Himalayas in Asia.

Alexander was successful in spreading the Greek culture to Asia, resulting in a new Hellenistic civilization—a blended Greek and Asian culture. His kingdom became linked in a vast network of trade and commerce, changing the ancient world forever.

Alexander is considered to be a military genius and one of history's most successful commanders. Many military leaders have compared themselves to Alexander the Great, and military academies throughout the world still teach his tactics today.

---

2. According to the text, what did Pericles do to improve Athens under his leadership?
3. What was the effect of Pericles promoting the arts and literature of Athens?
4. According to the text, why did Alexander conquer the Persian Empire?
5. What effect did Alexander the Great have on the ancient world?

6. **Writing Prompt:**

In your opinion, which is more important — to conquer or to build? In a well-organized essay, support your conclusion using Alexander and Pericles as examples and citing evidence from the text.

Ancient Greece Geography

Read the text and look at the map. Then use the text and map to answer the questions.

The geography of ancient Greece was mountainous, resulting in separation amongst people. Because people were separated, individual city-states were born. City-states were located in valleys between mountains or on coastal plains, and they controlled a certain area around them. As Greek city-states developed, they created their own language, culture, and identity. Athens and Sparta grew to be two of the major city-states of ancient Greece.

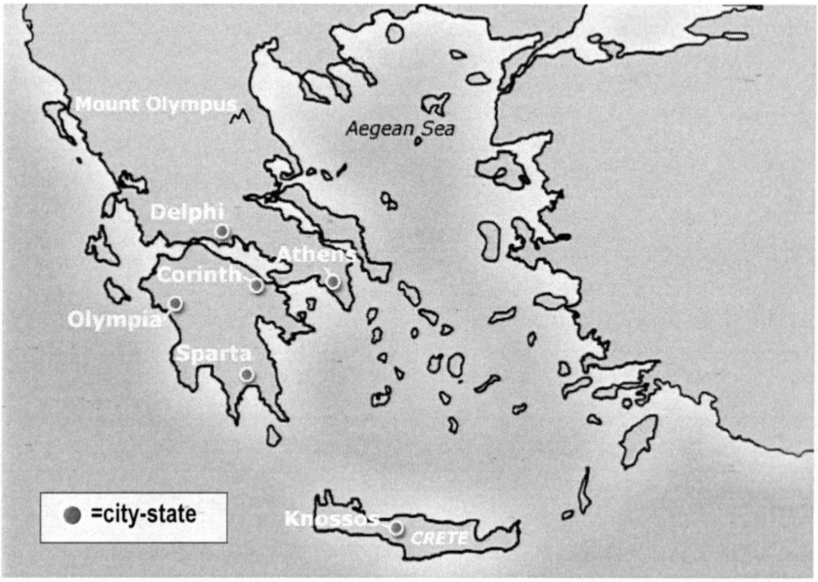

1. Use a dictionary to define city-state.
2. Circle the city-states shown on the map.
3. How did geography play an important role in the development of ancient Greece?
4. Communication between city-states was difficult. Use the text and map to explain why.
5. Geographically, what do all major ancient Greek city-states have in common?

Greek Prefixes and Suffixes

A prefix is placed before a root word to change its meaning.
A suffix is placed after a root word to change its meaning.

Use an online resource to complete the graphic organizer.

Prefix	Meaning	Example
anti-		
auto-		
bio-		
chrono-		
demo-		
geo-		
micro-		
mono-		
therm-		

Suffix	Meaning	Example
-gram		
-graph		
-ism		
-ist		
-logue		
-logy		
-meter		
-phone		

Use the combination of prefixes and suffixes to define these words:

a) biology
b) monologue
c) thermometer
d) geology
e) microphone

CHRONOLOGICAL EVENTS

History of Ancient Greece

Put these events in chronological order on the graphic organizer.

Greek alphabet is invented 750 BCE	Persian Wars 497-479 BCE	Trojan War 1250 BCE	Philip II becomes king of Macedonia 359 BCE	Democracy is born in Athens 594 BCE
Alexander becomes king 336 BCE	Cleopatra dies 30 BCE	Parthenon is built in Athens 447-432 BCE	Alexander the Great dies 323 BCE	1st Olympic Games 776 BCE

Ancient Greek History:

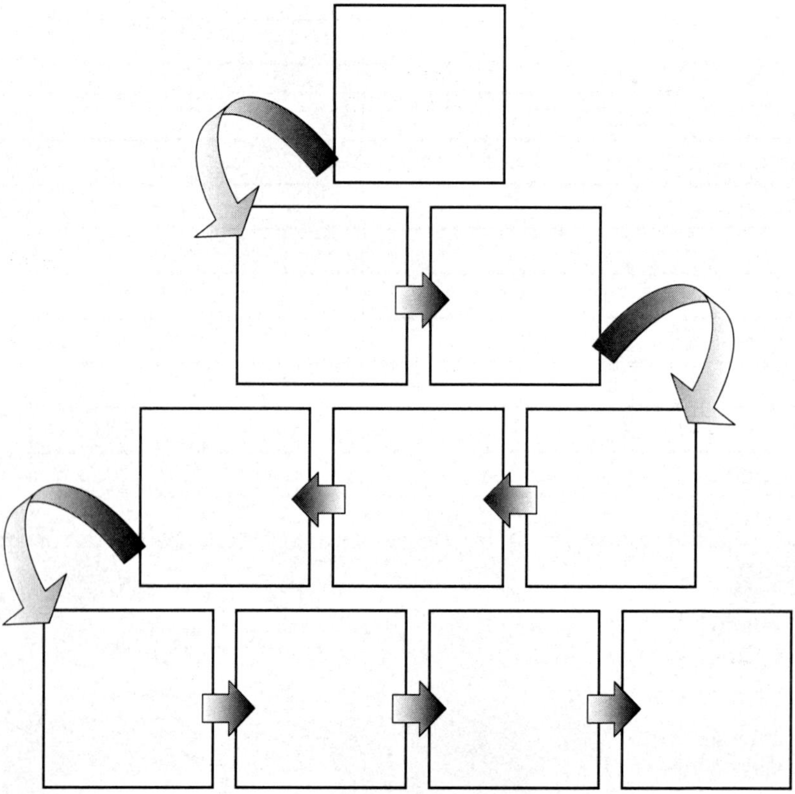

READING INFORMATIONAL TEXT

Trojan War

Read the text and answer the questions.

The Trojan War was a major conflict between the Greeks and the Trojans. The Trojan War lasted 10 years and is the source of many heroic stories.

The conflict originated when Paris, son of the Trojan king, kidnapped Helen, wife of the Spartan king, and took her to Troy. In return, Menelaus, Helen's husband and king of Sparta, led a voyage to Troy to save his wife. Many Greek warriors sailed to Troy to support their king. The Greeks battled the Trojans for ten long years, but the Greeks were not able to break through Troy's city wall using only strength.

Before leaving Troy, the Greeks left a giant wooden horse outside the city walls. The Trojans were surprised by the gift and dragged it inside their city. The Trojans did not know Greek soldiers were hiding inside the horse! During the night, the Greek soldiers climbed out of the horse, opened the gates to the city of Troy, and led the Greek army inside the city. The Greek army burned the city of Troy and overthrew the Trojans.

Tales of the Trojan War are found in many pieces of Greek literature and depicted in numerous works of Greek art. Some of the most famous examples are Homer's epic poems; the *Iliad* and the *Odyssey*.

1. According to the text, what caused the Trojan War?
2. According to the text, was the Trojan War important to Greek history? Cite evidence from the text to support your answer.
3. How did the gift of the wooden horse effect the outcome of the Trojan War?
4. Write a paragraph response supporting the statement, "Brains are better than brawn." Use evidence from the text.
5. How could the Trojan War have been avoided? Explain.
6. In your opinion, is it worth fighting an entire war for one person? In a well-organized paragraph, explain your conclusion.

Athenian vs. U.S. Democracy

Read the text and answer the questions. Then complete the graphic organizer

Ancient Athenian democracy developed in the Greek city-state of Athens around 550 B.C.E. Athens had a direct democracy, a political system in which the people voted on legislation directly. Only males of Athenian birth who were at least 18 years old were allowed to vote. Women, children, foreigners, and slaves were not considered citizens and, therefore, not allowed to vote. The population of ancient Athens is estimated at 250,000, but only around 30,000 people were citizens.

In Athens, all citizens held political power. The citizens directly created new laws and acted as judges. All citizens gathered together—usually in an outdoor area—to argue, debate, and ask questions before voting. Each person had an equal say (one vote), and the majority decided what the government would do.

The leader of Athens was chosen by a lottery system. In a lottery system, unlike the election process in the United States, a leader was chosen by random drawing. The Athenian executive branch was made up of a single council of 500 men. Furthermore, the judicial branch only used one-day trials with juries of various sizes—no attorneys and no appeals.

When the Founding Fathers created the American democracy, they included important qualities of Athenian democracy. However, the United States uses a form of democracy called representative democracy. In this system, the citizens do not directly vote on laws. Citizens vote for people to represent them in the government. In the United States, if you are at least 18 years old, registered to vote, and a U.S. citizen, you can vote, regardless of your race, gender, or religious beliefs.

In our representative democracy, U.S. citizens have the power to elect government representatives. United States' citizens elect many different representatives into government offices, including senators, representatives, governors, district attorneys, mayors, and even the president.

Representatives in the U.S. government are divided into three branches—the executive, legislative, and judicial. These officials represent the American people by making laws, deciding court cases, and issuing executive orders.

1. Define the following words as used throughout the text:
   A. direct democracy B. representative democracy
2. Explain why only 30,000 of Greece's population were citizens.
3. What is the relationship between ancient Greece's democracy and the United States' democracy?
4. How are the democracies of ancient Athens and the United States similar? How are they different? Use the Venn Diagram to organize your response.

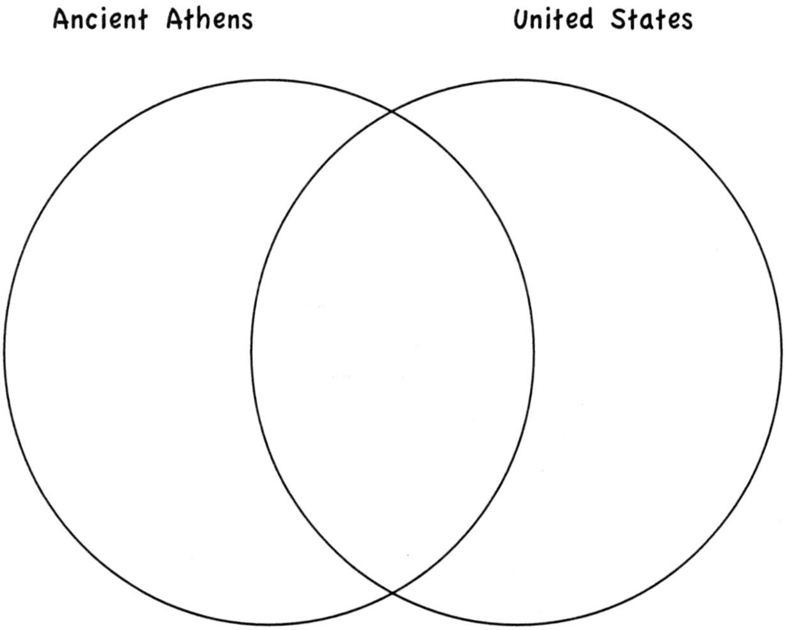

5. Which form of democracy is more effective — direct or representative democracy? Write a well-organized essay, develop a point of view, and support your argument with evidence from the text.

   As a class, discuss and debate your responses to the prompt. Expand your answers to the prompt based on the discussion.

Greek Philosophers

Read the text and answer the questions.

Greek philosophy focused on logic, mathematics, political thought, and science. Throughout the years, many philosophers began writing books about their thoughts. The most famous of those Greek philosophers were Socrates, Plato, and Aristotle.

Socrates is considered a founder of western philosophy. Socrates did not write down his teachings; therefore, he is primarily remembered through the writings of his student, Plato. Socrates is remembered for inspiring many thinkers and scientists to use reason to question the world around them.

Socrates' most famous student, Plato, was a philosopher, writer, and mathematician. He created the Academy in Athens, which was the first institution for higher learning in the world. Plato was a sophisticated writer who wrote books on many topics, such as philosophy and mathematics.

One of Plato's students, Aristotle, also became a philosopher, teacher, researcher, and writer. Aristotle is best known for creating a moral code for "good living." To do this, he used reason to examine human behavior in society and government. In addition, he tutored Alexander the Great as a young boy.

Greek philosophy was very important during ancient times as well as today. The philosophers of ancient Greece researched and wrote about many ideas that influenced the foundation of modern philosophies.

1. A. Use a dictionary to define philosophy.
   B. What part of speech is philosophy as it is used in the text?
2. Explain why Socrates is remembered as a founder of western philosophy.
3. List three ways Plato contributed to ancient Greek philosophy.
4. According to the text, how did Aristotle create a moral code of "good living"?
5. Explain the relationship between Socrates, Plato, and Aristotle.

Greek Philosopher Quotes

Rewrite each quotation to complete the chart. Use the completed chart to answer the questions.

Greek Philosopher quotes:	What each quote means to me:
"No man undertakes a trade he has not learned, even the meanest; yet everyone thinks himself sufficiently qualified for the hardest of all trades, that of government." –Socrates	
"One of the penalties for refusing to participate in politics is that you end up being governed by your inferiors." –Plato	
"Even when laws have been written down, they ought not always to remain unaltered." –Aristotle	

1. What is the common theme shared by all three quotes?
2. What is your opinion of each philosopher's point of view? Do you agree or disagree with Socrates? Plato? Aristotle? Use your rewritten quotes to support and explain your position in regard to each.
3. Choose one point of view to defend. Write a short speech to your class promoting that point of view. Present your speech to your class. Can your audience accurately identify your point of view?

Important Elements

Identify the main elements of ancient Greek civilization to complete the graphic organizer.

GEOGRAPHY

____

____

____

THE ARTS

ANCIENT

____

____

____

EDUCATION

____

____

____

# of Ancient Greece

RELIGION

GREECE

GOVERNMENT

CONTRIBUTIONS TO MODERN DAY ARCHITECTURE

Athens vs. Sparta

Read the text and answer the questions.

Athens and Sparta were the two most famous and powerful city-states in ancient Greece. However, they were very different in geography, government, and culture.

Geography

Located near the Aegean Sea in central Greece, Athens was built below the Acropolis, which stands on a hill above all of Athens. Athenians built walls to defend against enemies. In contrast, Sparta was isolated and located on plains surrounded by mountains, making it difficult for enemies to invade Sparta.

Government

Although both Athens' and Sparta's governments were elected by the people, they were quite different. The form of government in Athens was a <u>democracy</u>. Athenian democracy was based around a group of citizens known as the <u>assembly</u>. Only men born in Athens who were at least 18 years old were considered citizens.

In Athens, each citizen took part in the assembly where they debated and voted on laws. However, at least 6,000 citizens were required at each assembly meeting. Sometimes, slaves were sent out to retrieve citizens to attend the meeting. Additionally, a council of 500 citizens determined the guidelines of daily activities.

On the other hand, Sparta's government was an <u>oligarchy</u>, a government ruled by a few people. A group called the Council of Elders, made up of two kings and a council of 28 elders, ruled Sparta's oligarchy. Sparta's government also included an assembly. Only men were allowed to participate in voting and decision-making.

Economy

The center of Athenian life was a marketplace known as the <u>agora</u>, where goods were bought and sold. Because of the popularity of this form of trade, Athenians developed coins as a source of money. The agora attracted people from other Greek city-states to Athens, helping to spread ideas through travel, trade and building strong relationships with other city-states.

In contrast, Sparta relied on farming and conquering other people's land rather than trading. Spartans turned neighboring peoples into slaves called helots to work and farm their land.

Culture

Athens was known for its creativity in science, philosophy, and art. They believed in a good education for boys only. Boys were taught many subjects such as math, writing, music, reading, and physical education. At the age of 18, they attended two years of military school. In contrast, Athenian girls were not educated unless they came from a wealthy family. Girls learned domestic skills from their mothers at home and were not allowed to take part in anything to do with war, business, or education. They had very few rights and could not vote.

In contrast, Sparta was a society of fierce warriors focused on obedience and military strength. Spartan boys did not have to work or be educated formally, but they were trained to be warriors from age seven. There was no choice of what they would do when they reached adulthood—they had to join the Spartan army. Spartan girls underwent military training as well because they would grow up to be mothers of warriors. Although they were not allowed to participate in war, girls took part in the training because it was believed that fit women produced strong children who would one day fight. Spartan women also had many rights, such as owning property and speaking in public.

1. Define democracy, assembly, oligarchy, and agora as they are used in the text.
2. Who was included in the Athenian assembly? What was the assembly's purpose?
3. Identify the primary difference between Athenian democracy and Spartan oligarchy.
4. In your own words, how would you characterize Sparta? Athens?
5. On a separate sheet of paper, draw four Venn diagrams. Complete the diagrams by comparing and contrasting Athens and Sparta in each of the following areas: geography, government, economy, and culture.

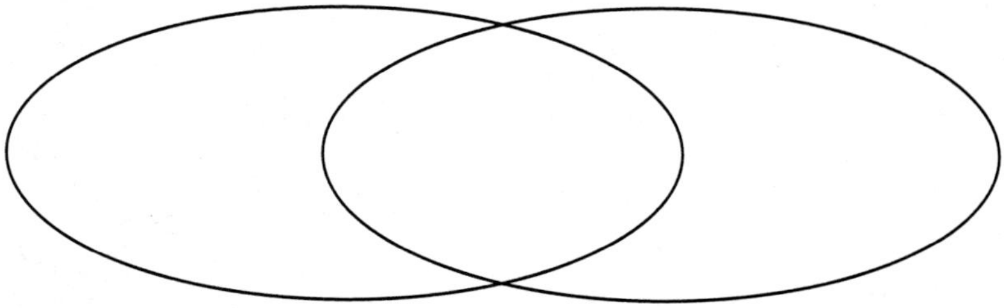

Ancient vs. Modern Olympic Games

Read the text and answer the questions. Then complete the graphic organizer.

The Olympic Games were originally called the "hunger games." They were a series of athletic competitions among representative athletes from many Greek city-states. The games began in 776 B.C.E in Olympia, and they honored the king of the gods, Zeus. Games were usually held every four years, and the city-states agreed to an "Olympic Truce" and stopped wars between the states during the games.

The games were always held in Olympia, and only freeborn, non-slave, Greeks were allowed to participate. The original Olympic Games lasted for one day, but eventually they grew to five days. Athletes competed in only a few events. Most events were track and field events. Over the years, more events were added like boxing, wrestling, and chariot racing. Victors were praised and honored with wreaths of laurel leaves to wear on their heads.

The Olympic Games became a political tool used by city-states to proclaim dominance over their rivals and to share culture and trade goods. The Olympic Games were also a celebration of religion and artistic competitions. The Olympics continued until 394 C.E., when the Roman Emperor ordered them to end.

In 1894, a Frenchman Baron Pierre de Coubertin re-introduced the Olympic Games after 1500 years of their absence. As a result, he is considered the father of the modern Olympic Games.

The first modern Olympic Games were held in 1896 in Athens, Greece. Unlike the ancient Olympic games, modern Olympic Games are not always hosted by Olympia, Greece. Every two years, a different city has the honor of hosting the Summer or Winter Olympics. The host city is responsible for welcoming all competitors and important visitors from around the world.

Today, the Olympic Games are a major international event that includes thousands of athletes in many different competitions. The modern Olympic Games are now split into two different competitions, the Summer Olympics and the Winter Olympics. The 2012 Summer Olympics featured a total of 26 sports and over 300 events, while the 2010 Winter Olympics only included 15 sports and 86 events. The modern Olympic Games can last up to an entire month! The winners of each event earn either a gold, silver, or bronze medal—for first, second, or third place.

The Olympic Games today are used to support fair competition between countries and to promote peace, cooperation, and good relationships.

1. List three purposes of the original Olympic Games.
2. List three purposes of the Olympic Games today.
3. What are the responsibilities of the host city of the modern Olympic Games?
4. In your opinion, did the modern Olympic Games make improvements to the original Olympic Games? Support your opinion with information from the text.

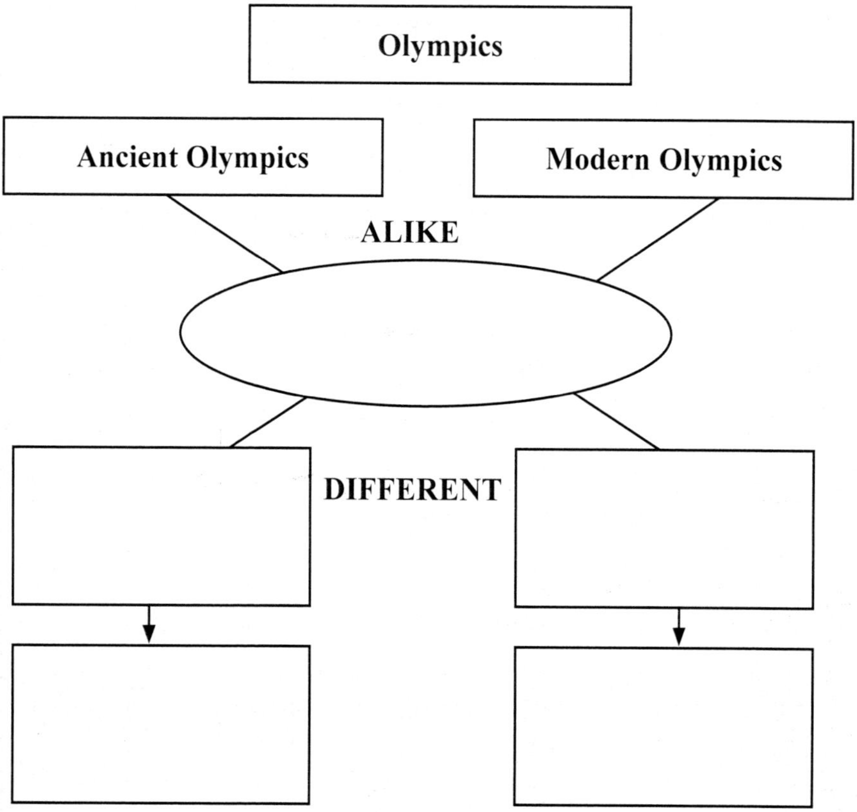

Greek Mythology

Read the text and answer the questions.

Greek mythology is a collection of stories and legends about gods, heroes, and the origin of the Greek people. Ancient Greeks used mythology to explain how the world works. The Greeks believed that the gods caused natural events, from the rising of the moon, to thunderstorms, to daily relationships between people. Greek gods like Zeus, Apollo, and Athena were often blamed for making people fall in love or for causing destruction. Each city-state had its own myths about heroes, real or fictional, who slayed terrible monsters. The most famous Greek hero was Hercules, who was given many tasks by the gods.

The writings of many influential ancient Greek authors include mythological characters and are still read today. Homer's famous epic poems, the *Iliad* and the *Odyssey*, told of Greek gods and heroes and have inspired writers for thousands of years. In addition, ancient Greek playwrights like Sophocles, Herodotus, and Euripides wrote comedies and tragedies about mythological characters that later inspired modern European theater.

Greek literature, language, and art have also had a great influence on modern culture. The English language has many words that come from Greek mythology. A "long journey," for example, is called an "odyssey" after Odysseus. Modern poets and writers often use Greek mythological characters, themes, or ideas for inspiration. Greek mythology is a great source of stories and themes that are still important and relevant today.

1. Define mythology as it is used in the text. What Greek root words help you identify the meaning?
2. Why did the ancient Greeks create mythology?
3. Describe how Greek mythology has influenced modern writers.
4. Use an online resource to research a Greek myth of your choice. Work in small groups to identify the characters, summarize the plot, and explain its significance in a well-organized report.

Athenian Agora

Analyze the map and answer the questions.

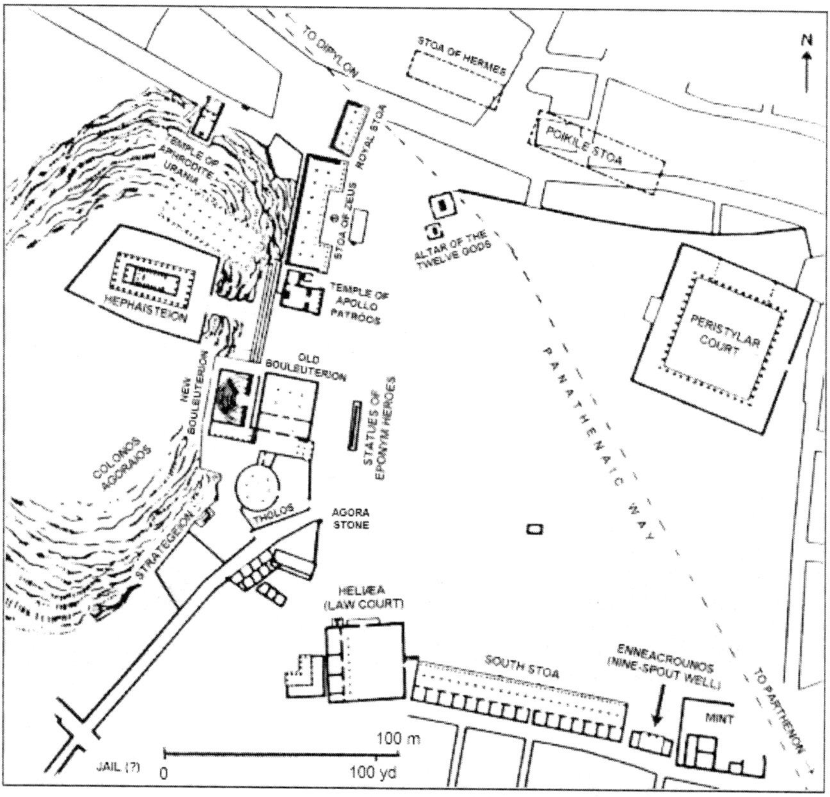

1. Use a dictionary to define <u>stoa</u>. What can you infer about stoas by the size and number of stoas in the Agora?
2. Estimate the total size of the Agora.
3. What is the significance of the path marked with a dashed line?
4. Look at each building name. What can you infer about the importance of the gods in Athenian culture?
5. Choose a building in the Agora. Use an online resource to find images and create a short oral presentation about the building's purpose in ancient Athens. Share your presentations.

COMPARISON OF PRIMARY SOURCES

Greek vs. Modern Architecture

Analyze the images and answer the questions.

Temple of Hephaestus in Athens

Erechtheum on the Acropolis in Athens

Ancient Greece

Temple of Olympian Zeus

Theatre of Dionysus

1. Compare and contrast the architectural buildings of ancient Greece and modern day.
2. What can you infer about the relationship between ancient Greece and modern day architecture?
3. What can you infer about the relationship between ancient Greece and modern day culture?

Modern Day

Lincoln Memorial

White House

National Archives & Records Administration

Baseball stadium

COMPARISON OF PRIMARY SOURCES

Speeches of Pericles and Lincoln

Around 490 B.C.E., Pericles, an Athenian leader, delivered a funeral speech after the first battle of the Peloponnesian War. In 1863 C.E., United States President Abraham Lincoln delivered a speech after the Battle of Gettysburg during the American Civil War. Even though the two speeches were given thousands of years apart, they share similar themes.

Read the quotations, complete the graphic organizer, and answer the questions.

Pericles' Funeral Oration	Lincoln's Gettysburg Address	Shared Theme
"I shall begin with our ancestors: it is both just and proper that they should have the honour of the first mention on an occasion like the present...And if our more remote ancestors deserve praise, much more do our own fathers, who added to their inheritance the empire which we now possess, and spared no pains to be able to leave their acquisitions to us of the present generation."	"Four score and seven years ago our fathers brought forth on this continent, a new nation, conceived in Liberty, and dedicated to the proposition that all men are created equal."	
"For it is hard to speak properly upon a subject where it is even difficult to convince your hearers that you are speaking the truth."	"The world will little note, nor long remember what we say here..."	

"Our constitution does not copy the laws of neighbouring states; we are rather a pattern to other than imitators ourselves. Its administration favours the many instead of the few..."	"...a new nation, conceived in Liberty, and dedicated to the proposition that all men are created equal... that government of the people, by the people, for the people..."	
"So died these men as became Athenians. You, their survivors, must determine to have as unfaltering a resolution in the field..."	"It is for us the living, rather, to be dedicated here to the unfinished work which they who fought here have thus far so nobly advanced. It is rather for us to be here dedicated to the great task remaining before us—that from these honored dead we take increased devotion to that cause for which they gave the last full measure of devotion—that we here highly resolve that these dead shall not have died in vain..."	

1. A. Use a dictionary or online resource to define funeral oration.
   B. Infer why Pericles would have given a funeral oration at that time.
2. In Lincoln's address, he refers to an event "Four score and seven years ago." To what event is he referring?
3. What is the shared tone of both speeches? Cite words/phrases that help you identify the tone.
4. Using inferences from the text, explain Lincoln's purpose for giving the Gettysburg Address.
5. In your opinion, did Pericles' funeral oration influence Abraham Lincoln's Gettysburg Address? Cite evidence to support your answer.

Correlations to Common Core State Standards

For your convenience, correlations are listed page-by-page and for the entire book!

This book is correlated to the Common Core State Standards for English Language Arts grades 3-8, and to Common Core State Standards for Literacy in History, Science, & Technological Subjects grades 6-8.

Correlations are highlighted in gray.

	READING	WRITING	LANGUAGE	SPEAKING & LISTENING
	Includes: RI: Reading Informational Text; RH: Reading History	*Includes:* W: Writing; WHST: Writing History, Science, & Technology	*Includes:* L: Language; LF: Language Foundational Skills	*Includes:* SL: Speaking & Listening
PAGE #				
2-3	RI RH **1** **2** **3** 4 **5** 6 7 8 9 **10**	W WHST **1** 2 3 **4** 5 6 7 8 9 **10**	L LF 1 2 3 4 5 6	SL 1 2 3 4 5 6
4	RI RH 1 2 3 **4** **5** 6 **7** 8 9 **10**	W WHST 1 2 3 4 5 6 7 8 9 10	L LF 1 2 3 **4** 5 6	SL 1 2 3 4 5 6
5	RI RH 1 2 3 **4** 5 6 7 8 9 10	W WHST 1 2 3 4 5 6 7 **8** 9 10	L LF 1 2 3 **4** 5 6	SL 1 2 3 4 5 6
6	RI RH 1 2 3 4 **5** **6** 7 8 9 **10**	W WHST 1 2 3 4 5 6 7 8 9 10	L LF 1 2 3 4 5 6	SL 1 2 3 4 5 6
7	RI RH **1** **2** **3** 4 5 6 7 8 9 10	W WHST **1** 2 **3** **4** 5 6 7 8 9 **10**	L LF 1 2 3 4 5 6	SL 1 2 3 4 5 6
8-9	RI RH **1** **2** **3** **4** **5** 6 7 8 9 **10**	W WHST **1** 2 3 **4** 5 6 7 8 9 **10**	L LF 1 2 3 **4** 5 **6**	SL **1** 2 3 4 5 **6**
10	RI RH **1** **2** **3** **4** **5** 6 7 8 9 **10**	W WHST 1 2 3 4 5 6 7 8 9 10	L LF 1 2 3 **4** 5 **6**	SL 1 2 3 4 5 6
11	RI RH **1** **2** 3 4 **5** 6 7 8 9 **10**	W WHST **1** 2 3 **4** 5 6 7 8 9 **10**	L LF 1 2 3 4 5 6	SL 1 2 3 **4** 5 **6**
12-13	RI RH **1** **2** 3 4 5 6 7 8 **9** **10**	W WHST 1 2 3 4 5 6 7 **8** **9** **10**	L LF 1 2 3 4 5 6	SL 1 2 3 4 5 6
14-15	RI RH **1** **2** 3 **4** **5** 6 7 8 9 **10**	W WHST 1 2 3 4 5 6 7 8 9 10	L LF 1 2 3 **4** 5 **6**	SL 1 2 3 4 5 6
16-17	RI RH **1** **2** 3 4 **5** 6 7 8 9 **10**	W WHST **1** 2 3 **4** 5 6 7 8 9 **10**	L LF 1 2 3 4 5 6	SL 1 2 3 4 5 6
18	RI RH **1** **2** **3** **4** 5 6 7 8 9 **10**	W WHST 1 **2** 3 4 **5** **6** **7** **8** **9** **10**	L LF 1 2 3 **4** 5 **6**	SL 1 2 3 4 5 6
19	RI RH 1 2 3 **4** 5 6 **7** 8 9 **10**	W WHST 1 2 3 4 5 **6** **7** **8** **9** **10**	L LF 1 2 3 **4** 5 **6**	SL 1 2 3 **4** **5** **6**
20-21	RI RH **1** **2** 3 4 **5** 6 7 8 9 **10**	W WHST 1 2 3 4 5 6 7 8 9 10	L LF 1 2 3 4 5 6	SL 1 2 3 4 5 6
22-23	RI RH **1** **2** 3 **4** **5** 6 7 **8** **9** **10**	W WHST **1** 2 3 **4** 5 6 7 8 9 **10**	L LF 1 2 3 **4** 5 **6**	SL 1 2 3 4 5 6
COMPLETE BOOK	RI RH **1** **2** **3** **4** **5** **6** **7** **8** **9** **10**	W WHST **1** **2** **3** **4** **5** **6** **7** **8** **9** **10**	L LF 1 2 3 **4** 5 **6**	SL **1** 2 3 **4** **5** **6**

For the complete Common Core standard identifier, combine your grade + "." + letter code above + "." + number code above.

In addition to the correlations indicated here, the activities may be adapted or expanded to align to additional standards and to meet the diverse needs of your unique students!